RUMINATIONS

RUMINATIONS

WILLIAM M. REDPATH

BARBERRY PRESS
Keene, New York
2025

Copyright © 2025 William M. Redpath

All rights reserved. No portion of this book may be reproduced or transmitted in any form or by any means, electronic or mechanical, including photocopying, recording, or any information storage and retrieval system, without written permission from the publisher.

PUBLISHED BY BARBERRY PRESS
Keene, New York
redpathw@tiac.net

ISBN 978-0-9647730-3-5 (eBook)
ISBN 978-0-9647730-2-8 (paperback)

Printed in the United States of America

—

Book Design & Publishing by Kory Kirby
SET IN PALATINO

In memory of my sisters Nancy M. Redpath and Jean R. Becton

With respect and love

*My inner and outer worlds move
amid thought and energetic patterning,
states of consciousness
and states of being.*

*Within a ruminating freedom,
I record and organize these sequences,
illumined by the framing insight that achieved poetry is
a form of meditation.*

RUMINATIONS

Against Incarnation

I
Is it against incarnation,
that we posit transubstantiation?
And some ordinary decent vector is somehow obversed,
or modulated, in a Bach sort of alternative riff –
a sequence of this, now that.
The first idea records the universal densification of energy
into matter, its combination.
Though I know there are precedents for my understanding,
I tend to think of spirit as coming down from on high,
maybe somehow having to do with gravity,
the infused, infusing density.

Spirit is what leaves the prone corpse prone;
in its essence, it characterizes as Source.
And, returning to itself, it goes up.
Yet some spirit remains within the decaying, unprincipled
whatever, also perfect.

Yet alternatively, the "movement" of incarnation
could be multifarious,
multitudinous, multidimensional,
like outwards from
a center, a nothing,
continually generating from each cell, each portion of cell,
like a cornucopia, an ultimate whirlpool chakra,
a black hole without its traumatic predisposition.

+ *(poem continues on next, even-numbered page)*

II

Transubstantiation, the second concept,
is framed within a narrative of
taking in, from an outside.
It declares that spirit/matter,
its combination,
is returned to spirit/matter –
to us –
spirit about which we have an idea.
Or an experience of being.
We get to see how the two,
spirit and matter, become one,
sense how one is divided into plurality.
Two sides of a same coin.
Same coin.

The closest we can get to seeing the moment we embody
is by juxtaposition,
not by opposition.
There are no opposites here.
Opposites are only appearances.

In order to achieve this meditational *tour de force*
is to suppose that bread and wine are not just
your ordinary Wonder Bread and Gallo
but are already spirit and matter, which then
gets absorbed or maybe not so exactly,
by our so-called bodies, mind/bodies,
into transcendent awareness of our Christhood, our
more often than not somehow Center.
Not bad for confounding the obvious.

How does the ingested become the digested –

does it slide over like a piece of Jello
across a plate: what was there is now, altered, here?
It's got to be a sacred moment, and one which we want to see,
or maybe we'll just take the money, the transformation, and run.
If we can see the moment, then perhaps we can intensify,
shape its power:
achieve greater, more refined focus, enlightenment.
Or better, honestly collapse in awe.
Or cement the alteration, the conversion,
so that we shall be changed. And keep the change.

If we are a mandarin wise person
And know what we are,
taking in the mind-body of an equally exalted mandarin
seems a waste of everybody's time.
No one is more perfect than are we; we are the thing itself.
Who needs more Christ energy when that is what we already are?
It cannot be a struggle between equals for more of God:
I am more godly than you, or you are more godly than I –
who wins that sibling fight?
Everybody loses every way.

We are participants in our reality, our ultimate reality,
and it is from this shared place that we begin to see who we are,
shorn and shriven.
Defenses dissolve,
even courage becomes remote.
Can we set a time apart to witness this flowing swirl?
This swirling flow.
Our viewing alters our viewing.

+

If only, by an idea, we can hold the truth,
beyond fact, and suspend it,
realizing the sacrilege in the service of facts.
Is this the truth?
(That's what we are going for.)

05/13/2015

Almost 69

After the Yales,
the Andover,
the Maplewood, New Jersey Boy Scouts,
the Reunions,
what my father bequeathed to me were the permanent
joys of Beiderbecke and Flagstad,
and reading aloud.
I still tell his jokes,
all delivered with his canny, ironic understanding of
social and personal detail,
if I can get them right.

As he was dying, the old, habitual
neurons, now boring even to him, noted the
bars of his cage,
like the elephant he and I watched
in the zoo,
obsessionally, ritually nubbing one corner post
with the soft, pudgy tip of its trunk
as it continually paced within its
steel periphery.
I witnessed an elephantine madness;
no, despair.

So what he left me, amid these riches
and was always with him,
was the shadow, the unfulfilled potential,

+

global and personal,
which was never reached
in his civilization.
Who would have guessed that
reaching one's potential here meant
pattern resolution?

In this shortcoming I join him,
for I see the shadow everywhere, and it pains me,
in myself, in others.
I am sensitive to pattern
as I enter each room,
like a fish seeking a hook.

After the honorary degrees, the culture,
the radical artistic achievements
of people we admire,
there is some untouchable core in ourselves
which, seeking change,
never, hardly changes.
This has been noted before.
Longing for connection, perhaps,
the touch, the moment of humor
or inspiration,
yet these do not alter some fundamental pattern
which needs yielding,
dropping away,
melting – transmogrification,
if you will.

We are patterns' loyalists,
carrying a burden
which is both ours

and not ours.
I tell my clients we are each the Christ Child,
picking up parental patterns whole,
sucking them in, as the world's.
And we hold them as if they were ours
(at some blended level they are hardly distinguishable from ours),
even though we are now aging and old.
The secret reason we cannot give them up
is that they are not ours
(nor were they patterns which belonged to the transmitting parents who
radiate them in every caress,
even though they do not wish to share,
transmit such toxicity).

Our intelligence – our brain does not know how
to bring these patterns
from our house to the curb
for pickup and recycle or discard.

Suspended above narrative,
these patterns are conveyed invisibly from ancient failings,
irrational Stonehenges,
traumata as apparently solid as Pompeii.
This my father knew.
"Do not be like me," he said to his son,
who walked and thought like him,
even as a young boy:
I swallowed him whole.

So I pick up the baton

+

and do not live the lie
as he, unsuccessfully, tried to do.
Within civilization,
his and the ones he affiliated with,
he tried to become hypocrite,
disintegrate,
susceptible to the latest alumni fad.
He was so discouraged.

Incompleting narcissist to the end,
his last weary words to me were:
"You stood by me some of the time."
It was a reversal of the way
the deathbed benediction should have gone.
This was his father's curse,
bequeathed obversely,
frontally, the failings of three generations
coming down to this: betrayal.
Yet it was his unremitting loyalty to the awareness
that there was something shameful,
shamful about all of regular education
as he and others had absorbed it,
a distraction from some Nathan-like,
Mather-like preoccupation with
the true apprehension of Godhead, perhaps,
which inhabited his deepest ironies,
his delightful stories.
What he said at last to me
he could have said to all of (Western) civilization.

We are distracted by our achievements
from the driving force
of our traumata seeking resolution.

Nothing in classical education helps
with this core transformation,
at the turning point,
where we beginners must make the homestretch run.
Our classical civilization only assists
to show our ignorance, our relative impotence;
and the repetitions of the patterns,
their sequencing, not even ceasing in death,
as we are reassured.
Worold without end.
The verbal centers,
even the visual centers of our brain, betray
the problem, waiting always in the wings
to emerge as soon as we have
collected our well-poised entrances.
At our core, we hope for skill, grace, and luck.

And we are surprised as we succumb to their immediate force,
illustrate, and are nailed by their power.
This my father, Laocoön, knew.

Undergraduate Yale now costs well over $45,000. per year
(actually nine brief months);
but who warns
these hapless, civilizing youths about this truth?
Some texts are better than others,
but we are moving into the realm where it appears
that what they get are not even questions –
even now, questions are beside the point.
Is this university civilization a dupe,
an expensive babysitting

+

marketplace of elaboration,
the ultimate bait and switch,
designed to render verbal, artistic skills,
but no integration?
Unhappily, there is a time in our development
when I think it appears more than less.
What a surprise, then, when we cannot uphold even the basic
tenets of democracy because we have no depth;
mostwise, we are mere victims of our certainty,
if our depth may even be called that.

The addictive fashionableness of what
even the best educations promise
can keep us from the cutting edge of our own development,
and this my father knew,
more than many of his peers.
In this, he kept a strange, angular faith.
He languished in collective memory, even lightly poetic,
unable to hoist himself
from Tristan's, Arthur's, or Amfortas' bed.
Encompassing, the always incomplete narcissism,
brain's love-hate of its word centers,
its percentiles,
the paradox which rarely sites us truly in confoundment
and wisdom.

Down, down the field we march,
with our blue banners,
our giant attenuated,
additive foam handmits high,
not able to maintain the democracy without,
much less within.
This my intelligent father knew,

and it hurt him, as witness,
as incomplete renderer of the tradition.
It is this hunt for the stilling moment,
free, transformed, uninterrupted,
and sustained,
which has driven
me to where I am,
attempting to cast off
all the civilized narrative garments
which are proffered.

I am my father's son, in this best sense of the term, and
if I were to meet him now,
as I do each day,
this is where my conversation with him,
wounded, incomplete, vain, partially, but crucially betrayed
by self and other, begins.

09/08/2008

Already Love

It is 8:30am and already love has gone,
an inward corner turned, as it does,
only this morning, from a casual comment overheard,
I notice how it feels,
better – senses,
the abandonment of love itself, by itself somehow.
Love is *sui generis*;
it is self-evident,
and something in this turning is not quite a turning away,
the way you'd expect it:
a lover rejecting you by shifting its face
and shoulders
to the side,
away from you,
no longer frontally.
This morning it is a mere shift,
like now, then then,
now and then
without away.
The abandonment is without away.
It remains a corner turned,
a pause where what was and what now is
can be seen as separate,
and ordinary.

12/14/2012

As the Wind Blows

As the wind blows, the rest follows –
the sails, the sailors,
the boat, the wake.

The wake:
the wind blows, and I
can tell how far I've gone,
how far I've come,
by the shape of detritus waves
pouring off the stern of my boat
for a time
until even they dissolve,
integrate.

Pushed, we follow the wind
and all is settled,
even when we tack against prevailing
streams of air.

Like leaves perusing a gust which blows them,
windblown, we settle to the ground,
to our rest.

The rest follows all,
but can it be that
death is not the wind.

06/2009

At Once

At once he was all I wanted;
subsumed in flames I almost could
not see the bush beneath,
which never dies.

Then, he turned away,
partially to return,
and now he seeks me again
in that rhythm,
the echo of the passion
but not.

I cannot do anything else but
sublimate. The hug, the tenderness,
but not the aroused desire to
devour and be devoured.
It is a union curiously shallow,
my boat apparently on the rocks,
but still rocking – not completely beached.
It is a contract I agree to,
placating a vicious, frightened society,
for myself, and for him.
Not quite to dismiss him.

Were he, like another, to turn to me
with greater desire,
his consort, mine. . . .
Now, I almost quite don't miss him.

10/2008

Be

"Be yourself,"
as if that task is simple.
In *The Young Victoria* Albert instructs
the ascending princess that in order to
play the game of monarchy,
a game she reenters late –
as late as adolescence –
so that she is not a pawn,
nor treated so:
she must locate her focus
not at the (hollow) crown,
but to an identity which transcends
the accumulations
surrounding being a queen.
The only way to carry the crown is to be centered
beyond crown.
His advice, "Be yourself",
is an individuating beginning.

"Be" somehow vocatively,
linguistically,
supports the insight that
being, not a self being,
is the priority.

"Be yourself" may imply that,
but it contains the paradox,

+

namely that self cannot be.
Only being is being,
when we lose hold of the agency of self
and just are.
Then, surprised, we glance at the mirror,
and see we may wear crown.

05/06/2010

Behind the Moon

You are not yet at the bottom of the pool.
I have agreed to meet you there,
yet you are in distraction,
with side orders of LSD, etc.
– not my priority.
Addictive.

The joke is not having sex with you,
it is that I am not the one you are looking for.
Even if we were to have sex,
and probably for a time
it would be healing for you;
maybe ok with me – after all,
it is the trusting moment I long for,
even with you;
it still would not be aligned
because of age.

The aftermath:
you could always retreat to our implicit ageism,
making it explicit,
and so could I.
We could keep from experiencing the full point.
Still point, full point.

I have been the person you have trusted most,
the person you have felt the safest with.

+

Now I am not sliced bread.
But with repeated firing,
I'm toast.

Respected most.
You are holding a burden which you need not hold, by yourself.
I go:
one shot or shots,
and then, I am told,
I must go behind the moon.

Two kinds of trust.

If you have felt abused, and you could easily play that card,
we all want to: God has abused us. Get a Job.
This is the wrong shot to play.

We are rushing forward to declare our unfairness,
our abuse,
and that is the first stage of the rocket,
but it quickly turns into smoke and mirrors.

Our intuition is that taboos are
tunnels of love,
where abuse can be reformed
in darkness,
phone booths where Clark
can transform into capéd wonder;
no other crucible will do
to dissolve this weighted, immobilized
despond.

We should see what it takes to revise and redress the injury –

perhaps a lifetime of contact,
an apology correctly framed,
the assorting of true responsibility,
which we (and God) engage together as
hovering hummingbirds,
in lifelong midair.
Sistine Adam and God.

According to the current rules I am now playing under,
I have one set of encounters with you,
a freebie, as it were,
in which to explicate my understanding of the agreement,
and we discuss it fully.
Then, depending upon your next moves,
I go behind the moon.
Do you want a relationship with me or no?

Your (is that possessive correct?)
addiction is a sidebar, side car, side show
from the main mea,
concealing
your still hidden stillpoint and
its surrounding, wagon-circled despair.

11/27/2009

Betrayal

How far beyond narcissism's
vast empire does
betrayal lie?

I think they are boundary-adjacent territories,
like Waltham to Watertown
or Palestine to Israel,
or envy, bright green on the map,
next to projection, awash in light purple.

06/2008

Be-trayal

So many times
the Conservative Commentator
on CNN torques what
the senator has said and shouts,
"Betrayal."
He doesn't listen.
He hears with his own ears,
his encapsulation so clear.
He has no question for the senator;
he assumes he knows what
the senator means, and by means,
he means a new chance to say, "No –
whatever you say, I say no."
He will deliberately smash the
spoken words against the wall
in partisan rhetoric,
as if this is the only way he can hear.

Bullied, he bullies.
The playground, second grade,
is his school and diploma.
Everything is elbowed out of the way.
Nothing is as important
as assuaging, surrounding,
agreeing to the domination of anxiety.
That is the level playing field he seeks,
like walking over marbles

+

on a concrete floor.
Betrayed, he betrays.

I don't know:
our strongest statement
made to God.
Perhaps It responds
the same.
The knowing says
that somehow
what is ordered
by our brain
is the same
for It.
To know God
means we are God's
creatures, knowing as
It knows Itself,
as we know ourself.
It is more than that.
Its Knowing is not like ours,
though when we know,
we get a glimpse of It.
Our vision, still – is
Mind of God.

02/2010

Beyond

It is beyond our sexual identity, even
the coursing neurochemical pleasure
we feel. And so, if we plan an identity as
a trip for which we are hormonally inclined,
destined,
we can create families and encounters of trust
to beat the band;

but seeing past this envelop, this corporation
which is a person,
means we can return to the identity

knowing Ultimate Reality.
Can we sing a clear tone?

All the heterosexual tones apparently have been rung: it is
as if the pathway is so well trod there is no
asking for its validation

unless you are in Spain
and your priest reminds you to think of God as you come.

But Reality is above personality,
above sexuality as we know it.
It is an austere single focus,
and all things focus upon Its void
for strength, for comfort, for reassurance

+

that there is no meaning delivered from ultimate reality.

Our capacity to focus upon this truth
means we can appropriate our humanity to our humanity
and not try to assign it to God.
Not from our clear-headedness.

This is an arduous but bracing clarity.
Our appetites, our attachments,
make only partial sense.
Our passions,
enthralled by intellect and hormones,
are all aimed toward some humane goal:
to bring satisfaction, cessation,
clarity to bear upon our experience.

All disassembly of these projects
restores us to the Godhead,
making it clear when we humanely are and
from what from its coils
we would set ourselves free.

Meaning is another shop set up for us to play at,
but God is not meaning.

It is above such recoil.

We use Reality to launder out our predilections,
our thoughts. It is there to Dissolve,
return us to Voidy Awe.

It does not care if we are gay or straight,
Jew or Gentile.

(We may.)

Educated or poor. Cancered or daft.
It is all up to us,
and to render our systems as beyond.

To God, our sacrifices glance off the water
like skipping stones,
and at last, sink.

05/2014

Butterflies Fill the Sky

If ever the world were to change,
say, its environment,
something fantastic,
like getting warmer,
it would never happen.

If suddenly it got so
warm that we were down to
our underwear,
and all the plants
and animals had to change
and some couldn't and
they would die – like in
ecological niches – trees, then
flowers then insects then birds, etc.
not in alphabetical order
or the order of species.

If suddenly – and others could,
I mean, change –
even though we could not,
if it were so that no things
were the same,
then butterflies fill the sky,
blotting out the sun
like a golden umbrella,
with tiny spokes holding out
the flattened canvas,
of their wings.

If, then, all the plants
and animals dead or changed,
then butterflies fill the
yellow sky with yellow.

05/2009

Calligraphy

My brush sweeps the paper floor,
gathering up the white;
ink saturates,
leaving black lines
forever clean.

05/2011

Changing Tires on Lunchbreak

I wish that tire men would the truth foresee
And not vain promise when the job be done.
To register their tried reality,
Not saying, "12 noon" when they mean, "Past One."

I poise awaiting snow tires to be set
Upon their rims, a gleaming balanced pair,
Suppressing skids on winter pavement wet:
Suspended rubber, treads and speed and air.

Why should I have to wait for these erelong
While students pile up in my classroom school
Not learning truth or wisdom, right from wrong,
And me, these men, transform into the fool.

Ah so, I trust where I will never learn:
and find tired men who have my time to burn.

11/2010

Dan the Treeman

Dan the Treeman has cut two expanded views
from my porch to the mountains,
and the vistas are awesome.
Louis XIV surveys a fresh scape of breadth,

as from his carriage,
this morning wigless,
he supervises the surveyors' lines
of fountains and follies,
planned plantings,
fabrications and nature,
and he witnesses.
All Empire leads to this moment
and from this.

And I think, here is what the trouble is about:
man giving himself something,
in royal denial of depression,
in revolt against a catastrophic world
chasing its own demise,
to found a space where
something can be seen clearly.
It takes a lot to line up the shot,
and why not before now?
Before Empire –
why not everywhere, all the time?
We know this empiric universality,
but we do not enter it. Why?
Wherein is permission given, or taken?

If money, power, doesn't lead to this viewing site,
this opportunity,
what is all the striving for?
What we cannot predict is whether or not,
having climbed the mountain,
crossed the sea,
we shall be able to appreciate, that is,
tolerate the sensation,

the elevation, the stillness,
the mystery
inexorably unfolding before us.
If I own the site of the view,
does that make it certain
I shall be able to witness what
lies before me?

I know we can garner this opportunity
on a golf of course,
gazing at paintings, words,
in sports or concert or religious moment,
making love,
comforting a child –
but I forget this occasion is
here all the time,
and this is what I lose,
all the time. Or we are informed,
but we don't or cannot listen:
the instructors themselves are so flawed.

+

The poised, arched moment
hovers above and around us,
but we are too busied
by ourselves and our plight
to be awed.

Yet our private neurochemistry is the civilization:
this is what exterior, boundaried gestures,
bridges, paintings, operations head toward,
the transformation and settling of
consciousness,
when the blur of subject and object
carries us beyond our
ordinary catalogue boundaries,
and we possess and are possessed.

The unconquerable moment
dissolves into radiance, and
all our automobile roads
lead here.

What books have you read,
what games played, songs sung,
what have you done with the leisure time
you have bought through diligence and focus,
postponing impulse?

We have spent hours and years
in creative and destructive endeavor,
and they keep leading to a moment,
(always the same?) when we are
(always) unprepared, unskilled,
trammeled.

Seduced by spectacle, I am
reduced to air.

Even Dan's skill takes me to the
momentary, momentous
promise of newness,
but I view the mountains,
and that is it.
Entire Civilizations,
Western and Eastern, North and South,
are reduced to a set of expanding,
contracting universes which I shall
scamper to somehow know.
Or not; and who can tell whether the impediment
can be fixed, or is not meant to be.

What will I learn from the view?
Those trained in philosophy and theology
will realize I have to move beyond cognition.
There is only the slightest chance that I can identify the sponsoring
view itself, much less my educated, disciplined,
differentiated response.

The moment: Can I know what it contains?
I suppose the shortest way to put it in words would
be, hopefully,
I shall witness the truth.
The truth of viewer and viewed.
The Truth.
Silent and vibrant.
To see reality in tranquility,

+

to share it –
to share responsibility with God –
some ultimate consciousness –
to trust.

Is this what Civilization entails,
and all its corrugation leads to:
a messy altar hastily acknowledged,
so that time itself can expand,
and with it, some small, trammeled eye,
destination, resting point for all light?
I am where light concludes.

Civilization involves the support of a set of singular
perceptual moments leading us appropriately to mystery.
The whirlpool tub, the toilet, the computer,
when asked to justify themselves, all plead,
"We lead to this moment,
unanxious,
hopefully open,
where open God and open I
can been experienced
and enzymes race their appointed rounds:
dancing as truth, and light.

I should not need Dan, or property,
or Michaelangelo
to frame the present for me,
though by creating pauses
they invite me to
hold my attention.
But not necessary; not.

Not worth the striving.

These fabrications, some more apparently essential
than others, lead to something.
They are merely they, and
they are not just they.

The manufactures which I buy and sell
lead only to the singular set of moment sequences.
The self which I propose leads only to
the singular set of moment sequences,
without wig, without self.
Each with its varied but essentially congruent
similarity.
No matter what the life-style, the politics,
the civilization,
its placement,
it is merely being support.
All roads, all vistas, lead to being,
and away.

08/22/2012

Dislocation

On an apparently hardly-noticed recent Nova program,
scientists show how Magnetic North is torquing into
Magnetic South,
a shift taking thousands of years;
and I turn
to see all of recent history
as a response to this
reorientation process.

I begin to wonder,
when did the
electromagnetic tremor
in the repositioning of
fundamental North begin to
be noticed,
or merely responded to?
Since World War II,
or I,
or the American Civil War,
the Revolutions,
the Reformation, the Renaissance;

Jesus,
the appearance of something thought to be in
the water drunk by Confucius, Buddha,
Lao-Tzu, the Sufi, the Zen Masters,
the Vedas,
Moses;
Our Lady of the Old Testament?

The beginnings of spoken language?

They say that the last shift of this
sort occurred 750,000 years ago, and
that before that, a similar reversal took place 200,000 years plus
beyond.

I see us charged within our molecular alignments,
which polar turning,
generations
regroup around,
subtly and profound,
attempting to stand
firmly, stolidly,
on the
authoritarian ground.

05/2010

Don't Fuck With Me

A corner turned,
and suddenly we, tender,
not fucking,
We're fucking,
fucking at
each other, at ourselves.

Surprised:
we –
by we.
Not fuck, no fuck.
Fuck with, not at,
Not fuck.

Fuck with,
No. No fuck.
No fucking.
Don't fuck.
Don't fuck at me,
Don't fuck with me.
Don't fuck with me.

05/2010

First Day of School

I wash my hands with hope,
watching myself in the glass.
I shall turn the door knob both
to the left and to the right
seven times
and climb into my suit.
Unlike smoothing wrinkles
drubbed in washed pants,
school holds no irony, no bored.

09/2006

Getting Naked With the Teacher

Perhaps more than once,
we have thought about it.
Most of the occasions lead to longing discharged,
or often to aversion and disgust,
the usual suspects.

The classroom setting sets us off –
it is charged with eros,
particularly when a grid of
structure or repression or taboo is
superimposed upon our raw desire to learn.
Our first teacher could be our lover,
or vice versa.

What occasions such fantasies is the
authority, the consistency of contact,
the desire to know the deeper truth about someone
who knows, expresses the somehow truth.
The integrity of the person who
exercises so much power over,
and more importantly, increasingly with us.

If teachers help unlock our power,
burgeoning as it is,
we want to return the favor,
experience full reciprocity:
we want the accouterments of marriage.
And yet, it is argued,
our imagined vision

is unreal.

Do we want to taste the specific skin,
the sorrow, the vulnerability about which
we know so little how to meet,
even the ecstacy?
After we have held one person
in orgasm, we've held them all, yes?
(Like nothing else,
such holding levels, maybe obliterates
the (authoritarian) playing field.)

Priest and acolyte, mystery is restored
and yet that is not our usual fantasy.
We do not say, "This coupling will end the power-tripping,
yours and mine, the exhaustion of masquery,
and restore Eden,
an unconscious, total awareness.
I shall experience experience with you,
treasured escort, and together,
we shall both
die."

Something there is that doesn't love;
a wall,
and you shall salve this wound,
and I shall heal yours,
held in such a way that that is all I have
been secretly waiting for.
God knows,
that is what it can mean,

+

getting naked with the teacher,
discovering an impossible, irrevocable truth
beyond becoming
or doing.

09/2011

Reverse:

What does the teacher have to offer the student? The revelation of his vulnerability, his ultimate truthfulness, his integrity, his fragmentation and his attempt to offer something whole out of that fragmentation.

His excitement, the cruising Dionysus finding its appropriate object, education. Let's keep the energy high so that it is distilled, not volatile, uncorrupted, with the body, but with distance. That is part of the lesson: the space. Then the attendance can be to its proper expression, beyond tests, learning, and expanding experience.

The taboo has not been examined, except it is always a new run, separate and reenforcing the parental taboo which is incestuous. The first incest is coming out.

Halloween 2013

I could not forget all the saints
while dressing this morning.
Each garment cleansed, repaired,
shrouds imperfectly my bulky frame.
But they, and I, will have to do.

Passing into light from light,
the transition is casual,
even when the first part of the rocket
drops away, mutely falling, like Sphinx – or Icarus?,
into some silent ocean
while the space pod rushes on its way,
and we have separation.

Buttons, socks achieved,
Each ungraceful moment filled with grace
Of which I may get a glancing glimpse.

Someone proffers the saints are my friends,
but saints barely look back – or to the side.
They are always facing forward,
aimed, without urgency, for center.
When I am with them,
I sense their sacred, harrowed journey, they mine.
Their heat becomes almost
collegial warmth, like geese gaining
supporting strength from flock formations for

+

the long, poised migration.

If you really knew me,
even better than I do myself,
you would know just how saintly
burdened my trajectory is.
The smallest soul struggles to fly free
amid debris and refusal.
Each moment.
Each tiny bird is witnessed because
it maintains some level of integrity
admirable: within and against torment,
perhaps within even a child-clear path –
who escapes sainthood?

Yet we barely see – not even the half of it.
What if we decided to show
what is here, within the complex moment
we trippingly call the self,
we would descend below, costumed
or perhaps naked,
to realms of assembly
beyond words,
where ideals are discarded,
not just negatively stated in
the form of demons or skeletons.
Obversely, the moment of sainthood
here cannot be observed:
only where we are one,
with no need to witness,
but to see.

10/31/2013

Halloween 2014: 6 for the day

Vampyres

World without vampyres
Is world without blood feeders:
Redding one-way streets.

10/31/2014

Halloween Stuff

Stuff means Halloween:
When bric-brac junk awaits
Transformationing.

10/31/2014

The Dead

Let the morbid rise
and float under toxic hot air balloons,
baskets of tourists beneath
their drifting globes.

They cling to the strings which
hold the platforms above
the smalling ground,
descending while they ascend.

What hope is here
in the air?
Their dolefulness holds
within the globe,
within the breath.

We've colored the balloons
orange and black, to
show we mean business,
but this is such a lovely
autumn day,
we're likely to forget.

And my spine chases itself
up and down, in gold.
I ease into this new berth
like a liner to a wharf,

+

creeping slowly, steadily,
momentum tiny, ship huge.

Black and orange are
the colors amid my brain,
signs of transformation.
Halloween is not obsolete
nor exploitable.

Let the others, not morbid, celebrate
in their way.
What do they know?

10/31/2014

I Have No Clue

I have no clue, for
Halloween secrets thrive, no
matter what the gear.

10/31/2014

Pumpkin

I don't want to be
A pie, baked and spiced: just
Let me be pumpkin.

10/31/2014

I Wake

I wake to scan turbulence,
a black cloud festering
and roiling,
some picture within, about my head.

I am happy.

I do not like the fearsome invisibility:
Fear means not seen.
If we see, then we understand,
and fear retreats,
like the Fundy tides
racing back into the sea.

This roiling is new, and with it
a visible site bringing clarity
to my screen.

It is only a matter of time
before the darkness dissolves.

10/31/2014

He Took

He took the teacup from her hand
and by doing so,
reformed her world.
No one before had lifted the yoke
from her shoulders,
the agony of responsibility
for which she was ill-prepared
and insufficient.

"Let me take this burden from your grip,"
the loving, the embrace;
"Can I set you free?
The task shall be mine."

She lay back and let him
carry the teacup to the counter,
where he set it down,
pristine, fully cup.
His fingers moved with care,
and for these moments,
she was free to move,
even to stay still.

Gravity lifts and draws us down;
we age,
our ability to respond to its force
draws blood
away from heart
into our feet.

Standing is an extraordinary balance
of countervalent vectors.

I am amazed that
sensate life configures so
at our fingertips, our extremities,
the longest distance
for the heart to feed.

I reach out and touch
and lift the cup from your fingers, and
I see your need,
your necessity,
and the impossibility here of
doing things alone.

Grace
trembles from heart
to fingers and back – a loop,
a lesson learned from
its handle,
curving away and returning
to cup's flank.

02/07/2008

I Come Into the World
to Touch

I come into the world to touch.
Implantation within the uterine wall means to connect,
and umbilical breathing begins;
it's to touch.
We no longer have to hold our breath.
I breathe to touch.

Breath is our experience of touching,
which we note when we sing, or are sung to.
We can hear when the breath, our touch, is compromised;
it is as if we are not to live.
And when our sound touches the far reaches of our soul,
we breathe.

06/05/2014

Icon

There are public figures, troubled, whom I want to rescue.
I think I want to be the one who standing by,
provides the presence
which stills their torment.
My desire to connect is linked
to the desire to save, or
as one who after all the disappointing others,
is truly capable of finally making the difference,
who knows there is a difference
and that it can be made.

Otherwise,
if desire,
and the desire to save goes to no such purpose,
why cultivate my own sensitivity?
Here is the seductiveness of charisma
(and these historical public individuals are herein ineducable).
I know at some level that there is a true selflessness in this
not-sacrifice.
And realistically, for my own peace of mind,
too near the blasting noise
of their demonstrating,
presenting personalities,
I want their volume to turn down.

And I know I thus repeat trying to save
my father from his incompleted narcissism,

+

which I did for a while
until he was overwhelmed by his own process
and drowned.
Yet I know that being a savior

brings problems with it.
Evoking healing has its tricks
and risks.

Perhaps such a good deed of accompaniment
will go unpunished
but probably not.
More likely unrecognized, unacknowledged;
I wouldn't mind that at all.
Here, total invisibility may be the very best way to go.

What is it I want to witness with these popular personality icons?
I must experience the disturbance
as disturbance, not attraction.
For example, the downhill speed-skier Judy Garland,
in desperate need of her bindings tightened,
evokes in me the desire to get a screwdriver
and wrench. From behind my spread fingers
I have watched her soar, and crash,
and I do not stick around.

But Marilyn Monroe,
or Vincent Van Gogh,
here's a pair for you
and for me.
It's mostly deeply married pillow talk
which fills my heart with them.
I am lying by each one's waxened side,

we holding, say, post-orgasmic court,
where they, and I, can finally be soul-quiet;
when the performance, the defense,
has not yet reassembled from its ego-shattered
location (in downtown Phoenix?),
for the next assault.

Monroe's eroticism has despair written all over it,
only in my adolescent preoccupations,
I did not understand that till it was too late.
You had to see past her breasts, her eyes, her mouth . . .
to her fearful barrenness,
and the barrenness of those who kissed her special feet.

Vincent is another.
No matter they write self-pitying,
self-congratulatory songs for him:
"We, not they, truly understand you."
Just like I want to say.

I tell my students
it is one thing to slum
in Vincent's awesome neurochemistry from afar,
on a wall
of a museum which is solidly built
and from which you can exit.
It is very much another thing to live intimately
with the daily, monotonous momentary disturbances,
truth's thread painfully stated, obscured, and torn,
as pigmented fingers lift the absinthe in a bottle,
the mood swings amid fingers

+

colored by fumous, brain-toxic pigment,
the stinking,
withdrawing roars,
the recombinant absinthe with the fingered failures to hold and be held.
Only his brush gets his best.

I will hold and kiss you, stubbled Vincent;
I will do more than that.
I will hold you not in awe, but until your iconographic recedes,
your childhood sketched past recognition into invisibility,
just like your paintings,
and there is no one left on earth but you and me.
We shall abstain, drink only sensation
until we settle down,
and seeing, finally witness.
And nothing special but the shared ability to focus together,
as you focus before the easel, solitary.

These days, budding stars seek swirling, ascending icon status,
raising some feature of their being into density
until a butte of color rises up off the canvas plain.
And through history their shadows lengthen
around Golgothan Ridge,
but they become distant, deliberately regal,
and of course,
on supermarket magazine racks,
they are tortured, and they fall.
Their trajectory is adolescent,
like reinventing void.
But some gestures frame our cultural scanning consciousness
and fix, and a mystery is declared,
even though we think we know what is happening,

like Veronica's hand adjacent to a Cross,
or Monica kneeling before the President.

Some say Vincent sends his ear to the woman who apparently has rejected him,
a mute, mural Madonna mounted on a monastic mosaic.
With prostitutional compassion, she remarks,
"You say you love, but I cannot hear what you are saying to me."

Somehow, his severed cartilage is between his fingers.
He smiles, in layered irony.
"Hear," he says, "hear: take, listen with my ear,
and perhaps you will understand what you don't."
He knows she is caught in her own iconography,
of her gestured self certainly (after all, she is a whore),
and maybe, in some terrifying moment, also of him;
he lives near but not too near;
here is a distance;
and in his madness he wishes
for her to be free of such auditory blindness,
for herself and for,
dare we say,
and with,
him.

Vincent does for her what I am doing for him,
offering to break through proposed, statued self
to essence,
from activity to essential action: and hold.

+

With the same, preverbal breath as is Jesus crucified on the Iconic,
Vincent's is a supreme act of chivalry,
like Raleigh throwing his expensive cape
onto the filthy street mud,
before the poised Elizabeth.

05/06/2009

I Lay My Flesh Down

I lay my flesh down
between pillow and bone.
What shall sustain me
while others carouse
happy in their encaging systems,
not a wise man among them.
Them.

Forget, forget,
the state of the art
to shed the garment paradox
and naked enter the heart.
The task takes
a framing, two weeks
or a day,
to find where the
New Year can
founder and play.

I watch the twins bicker,
now thunder, now blitzen;
and hope that the children
will die and be risen.

Hope, hope is movement surely –

knowing how many Pandas remain,

+

that makes them more tasty.
The fewer the Pandas there are,
the better they taste.

2010

I'm Good With My Hands

"I'm good with my hands."
Yes, you are;
and more power to you.
In your embrace
you hold the world
like a lover – suspending
lightly its essence,
with reverence for its
responsiveness,
its delicacy,
its clarity.

Your hands are the extension of your soul,
weightless, poised, fingered,
wristed,
and armed.
Your hands carry the firmness out
from under the irony, the smile,
the chuckle.
You are good with your hands;
with your hands you are good.

06/2009

Hell and Forever

Hell is not built of mistakes
but of longings,
blossoms suddenly sealed,
abruption forever repeated,
a land of irresolution,
nothing eternal about it.

09/05/2015

I Now See

I now see the suspended aspect of human life,
above death's floor,
meaning systems floating, zapping,
and if they fall, they pass through nothing
and dissolve,
water hopping, steaming on death's griddle –
I see this clearly, no longer my secret,
or my only vista
somehow held in the wrong way.

No, I've got it right,
and I hover to find out what I can or cannot do
within this suspension.
In the past I would withdraw, withhold,
realizing that nothing meant anything at all.
If you made connection,
it was pro-forma comforting,
transient and no matter how lucid,
compromised by
the space through which we fall into death;
it could never be denied, wiping out all meaning
with that single stroke.

People in the Twentieth Century said,
"Well, give connecting a try anyway,
make the connection,
commit

+

in spite of the void
and the cancellation platform
below that.
That is where the meaningless meaning gathers lustre,
magnitude. That very thing adds burnish to
the comforting commentary which
for a time reassures and assuages."

But these tightrope air hoverers:
some think the floor is support,
the space somehow not significant.
They do not draw their breath into it,
into them.
They do not look down,
not the steady, repeating way I do.
They do not clear the vision
of its densities
so that void can be seen, experienced.
And through that, like a lens,
view death.

09/2012

I Wonder How

I wonder how to guestimate the snow:
in numbers, size, or shape –
with so many flakes dropping, it is hard to
render calibration except in perceptual generalities.

Each
snowflake, sparrow, falls,
and for once I would like to know,
say, within the next moment, starting now:
what is falling – exactly, per second.
Per instant.

Does God know how many flakes:
God is above such pretty science.
God counts but does other things at the same time,
so It doesn't ever count.
By definition, It is the count.

Looking out, I might see maybe a million at a time
spaced one inch apart.
That's from my human levels of visual and conceptual resolution.
Each flake defines a space and
hits the spheroid earth like light hits the eyeball.

Snowflakes are not the last word in vapor,
any more than light is the last word in energy;
but because it hits the eye, light,

+

perhaps returning,
perhaps running somehow parallel,
stops in us, its vessel.
In me, light returns to light.
Light passes further to our sides and streams above, but
here in me as I witness, it appears
curiously
to stop.
Or pause:
this is what a moment is.

So with the snowflakes.
What I see is at some macro, always macro level.
My inner eye knows there is more,
trillions of atoms making up the single snowflake
and its surround, but my intelligence, my eye
resolves only at one (maybe two) level(s).
Politicians know this limitation, mine.

If I change my lens, like the eye doctor,
"Which is better, this lens, or that?"
I truly don't know how to respond.
It all ends in judgment, an hazardous place to
rest when it comes to truth.
I only get the answer concealed in my question.
Seldom beyond.
And seldom beyond the light.

Every cognitive call means I see what I can see,
not what I cannot.
I know I see more than I am aware of.
Perhaps I see everything;
but I do not perceive everything.

Every image, minute though each is,
is a somehow selected stopping place,
a garnered pause,
no matter what my rumination.

09/20/2012

Last Crisis

When all our secrets are uncovered, stored,
and made retrievable,
when we have been laid bare,
our barrenness exposed,
what will this stateless state of personality be,
without our privacy?
Our privacy does not mean our process addictions,
our secret pleasures.
Gradually, those will be accepted,
located as recognizable on the cultural landscape,
borne away in talkshow, webbed conglomerate,
somehow forgiven, retained,
and resolved into evaporating dew.

What will our personal room look like,
the one we enter
as we lay our head upon the pillow?
Uniform hiddenness no longer fragmented
by occasional illuminating beams of
flashlight, abrupting the darkness,
always with outline silhouette;
this will be broad, shadowless, uniform daylight,
lit from sides and underneath as well,
our closeted demons, like vampires,
chaste, escorted into withering, longed-for dissolve.

Small devils, who have organized our daily calendar
like competent executive secretaries,
will slowly explode

into new synaptic connections,
harbinging enlightenment we surprisingly might welcome,
like Zeus to a new, well-born Athena.
Do I want to be totally forgiven?
Totally known?
What if my fullness is immeasurable,
infinite?
Without corners,
what surprise is there in that?
I thought that knowledge came after,
not here on earth.
How dependent I am upon swaddling secrecy
to organize what I know about who I am.

If the outside (always) knows me better than I know myself,
without secrets,
what have I left to offer the person standing before me?
Turnéd nakéd, what is left to love?
If there are no veils with which to seduce,
what is left is mere sustained revelation.

If the world is always more compassionate than I am,
not even sullyingly, sullenly sadistic
in hidden pocket,
chest-strapped beneath its shirt,
tight like placental bonding,
what then?

Obviously, what is hidden about me is not
what I hide from others, but what
is hidden from myself – self, the ultimate secret,

+

secret mail-carrier.
I think, therefore I dissociate.
I think, therefore I conceal.
My privacies cast abroad for all the world to see,
silly secrets rut-jam for the Enquirer,
and I am somehow not here,
even where I am certain I know.
Now I will have enforced self-knowledge,
including void, at my center.
Everything else is taken away.

What if this is the last crisis of the soul,
that its embodied narratives are not important,
each bold sin just another ruse, a delay,
an illusion which keeps Hell active and important;
only with light, Hell evaporates, too?

Tell me how an animal can be a saint.
How can a saint dissolve into just what is?
No wonder we are confused,
making this relentless revision, a forced march
without footnotes,
with only gradual ascending dawn,
whose glance may fill my room.

06/20/2010

Leave Taking

The leaves take leave of the mother tree,
sliding, remaindered, through the wrap of air
until they, they hit the ground.
So shall I be grateful for gravity,
still constant amid changing climate,
intensified weather – why does *that*
come as a surprise?

I barely see the connection. I ignore my past in my present.
Nevertheless, here is harvest, including
not only fruition, but withdrawal, the leaf
shells – so soon transformed from living, breathing
organs into mesmerizing, unprepared for color.
Why do the reds and browns, yellow umbers, salmon pinks
come as a surprise?
If we change, we can stay the way we are.
Taking leave of the summer, the spring before,
the winter – and pausing, holding time still
before descending through the wrap –
why should this come as a surprise?

                                                            11/25/2014

Left Over

He wanted me to be like him.
In the old time, he said, "We are the same."
"We are not the same," I said.
Here we both speak the truth.

But he did not really want me to be like him.
"Don't be like me," he cautioned me more than once.

If I were to become just like him,
he would not trust that.
If I became too much like him, he became competitive.

Could he say,
"I, too, follow my father in the same way you do."
He never said that.

We could have talked this way,
murmuring, across a table,
perhaps between chairs in the library.

"How much variance or freedom
during the day do you have?"
"You have gained how much freedom?"
We could compare
and share.

The option for separation
is not an option. I run right up to his skin, and within.

When I was a young boy,
my mother was disturbed that I was so totally imitating him.
I did not seem to have any judgement;
reckless boy. He loves his tormented father so much.
To be is to be what is left over,
the self that is left
when everything, father and all, is gone.
That which is left when
everything is gone.

He stood on his father's shoulders,
but the task was to emerge into himself,
a task his father had not completed
but expected him, his son, to.
In that they were alike.

The same.
But the same is not the same.
Being is not the same as anything.

09/2019

Left Over Annex

If he followed his father as closely,
had my father ever individuated from his father's patterns?
Had I ever done the same from mine?
In that we are the same, the same question,
perhaps the same answer. Three men.

That is what I would ask him, were he here today:
"How much from your father's pattern could you vary,
could you extend your reach?"

Was the lineage of servitude,
of verisimilitude, carried
untouched unaltered from generation to generation,
with only a few steps taken beyond that line?

Was that what a father could be, the man who held the line
about stepping over it, over the past,
or was that only for American fathers?

The initiating moment has a huge undertow,
a conservatism which is natural and immediate,
and unquestioned.

To alter that is to what?
Step past recognition,
past affiliation, past bonding,
past plain old reality.

04/2012

Light Change (a portion)

Death brings out the worst in me,
the fear, the avoidance as I step off the curb
before the light changes.

10/2019

Mary Weeps

Pieta – she weeps for her Son,
an egoless agony,
mirroring with her own
his downward turning chin,
blood from the gushing forehead
purpling his carpet beard.
She has delivered a ball of sensation,
including tragic pain;
out of betrayed Conception,
into a betraying world.
If we are perfect,
everything is betrayal.
When we are perfect . . .

Why do it?
She is unthinking
as sperm journeys,
as the neonate crowns.
There is no choice,
the myth tells us,
tells us where we always are,
no matter what the story variations.

There is this connection between
being impregnated and being pregnant,
which somehow occurs,
but the gap is as large
as creation itself.
We must stay in our human

refusal of causation,
that which we seem to have mastered
but, upon reflection,
have misapprehended,
or missed.
Better to call the whole matter stainless
than to see our disconnect.

These are the facts of life.

The child grows, in strength and wisdom,
fathers me,
and wanders in a series of combinant reality,
of sameness with me and feared difference.
The sameness, maybe we can learn from that;
the difference, it is probably inconsequential.

I squirm within his forcepped reality,
trying to pry him out of his mother's locked, anxious womb,
aiding him,
finally letting him find his own way,
far from my control.

A small movement within my psyche manifests,
and maybe I have got a change,
one which will let me see myself
as separate and connected,
always that.

I peer down at my Birth Canal,
coaxing this fathering child,

+

no longer pulling,
allowing him to work with his mother's terrified muscles,
my work now,
I am both him and my grandmother,
so that it can be accomplished
and the full truth be known.

If I let him go, sink or swim,
he reassures me he will – something.
Sink probably.
His fear is more important
than the actual outcome.
The tragedy will solve itself.
In a moment –
the next moment.

I see him locked, unlocked,
Then locked again – relegated
as if by some Divine Whim.
I troll the complex grief for the chance to see:
my father never cried for me,
not as I have for him.

09/14/2009

Musée

Wystan, how right you are about suffering,
how it occurs when something else,
some radical encapsulation, is,
apparently, spinning within its own orbit,
caring less about the martyr
burning at the stake.
No matter what, indifferent Nature carries on;
the cat hunches in the litterbox.

Lots of paintings
demonstrate characters in a myth
desperately witnessing
a sinking ship,
a crucified man,
in agony and prayer:
Mary, Simon,
or the patron from Peoria, who joins
the painted crowd at the bottom of the Cross,
because he wants it identified that he attends
the suffering,
and, loyally, understands it.

But you note how Bruegel shows that the
environment's sympathy, not to mention its
empathy, appears limited, and
dual.
Have we then two orbits,

+

that of the sufferer
and that of the broader cloud of unwitnessing?
The plowman and the boat and the indifferent sun
are turning away,
or just not paying sympathetic, not
to mention empathic, attention.

That's for days when we witness
the suffering
and distance ourselves from it,
for our own reasons.
There is a line between me and the next person
which divides,
yet there is a line which connects
and remains forever invisible.

Re. suffering: Buddhists would seek out its source
in our attachment
(something separate from pain, to be sure).
We are not merely gazing at Icarus'
fall, the acceleration which may have his
eyes popping out of their orbits,
lungs locked and suffocating
amid so much air
as the body accelerates according to Galileo.

But Wystan, you too fall victim to your own insight.
"Icarus" contains one small speck,
that of Daedalus making it safely,
this time without his son.

Here are tears.
Flesh of my flesh,

the father has anticipated the folly of his youth,
and we are thrown in that moment
to consider how altogether little can be learned
between generations,
even when the advice is very good;
once the important information
has been silently, invisibly imprinted.

Above the land, now,
Daedalus slowly, carefully
drops to the safe, inhabitable ground,
ankles hobbling a bit
until he gets the feel of how to work the
wings with his feet and legs,
to be able to stop.
It is his first landing.

He turns back to face his future,
alone, as every parent must as we face death,
but without the comfort of genetic transcendence.
He has not had time –
maybe like an eagle,
he could have raced underneath
his wingless fledgling and caught him up
on the shoulders of his outstretched wings,
to drop him again and again until the tiny bird
learns how to fly, or grows real wings.
Maybe his personality was not forceful
in the right way,
to ensure success.
Maybe, maybe; the suffering begins with maybe.

+

And the self-pity.

Is the myth of Icarus in essence
survivor Daedalus' story?
He remains with an overwhelming sense of
success and loss,
something beyond what his magician's inventor's mind
can encompass.
If we see that in any suffering we are both its victim
and its instigator, that in our suffering
there is a portion of ourselves which does not care,
sailing calmly on . . .
Why not? Our elaborations are at the flood,
our grandiosity unchallenged.
What did we expect?

***

An Orthodox Jew sits shiva for his yet living son Abrahm
because Abrahm has been found to be gay.
Again, the son is sacrificed
by the father
to the grandfather's faith,
with no intervening pascality lamb between.
Soaring, the father will justify,
"I am afflicted Job,
no matter what J– throws at me,
I shall remain true to Him,
even at the expense of my son."

Who now can fly safely
across the Icarian Sea?
Who shall forget, nay, abandon a living trust,

at any cost,
to keep our faith,
perhaps because our fathers have not
taught us how to rightly read?
Our grieving shall be
circumscribed, like a blade paring
around some skin.
Here the ritual confirms:
we learn nothing
from the cut,
the cuttings.
What's to learn?

12/2009

Must I

Must I shatter all of civilization if I seize within your arms?
That would seem to be the gist of it,
all the cards stacked.
The ability to sublimate, gone,
all my former teachers, escorted against their will
onto the pillow, into the folds of skin.

My father also,
his fear, which motivates me,
whose pattern propels me
into your embrace.
What do I expect to see?
Our accomplishment is many faceted,
our ship is quickly backing away from the dock
and sailing out of the harbor,
to the sea which remains only partially charted.
We are past observation.
She has taken her mother's barely hidden pattern
and manifested for her,
not for herself.
All homosexuality comes from our parents,
not of ourselves. We do it out of generosity,
not need.
Does it come from the parent of the same sex?
It is not because of what we want from them,
but what we want to take on for them.

All categories are not our own, not finally.
Who is being served?

If I let him go
he may land on his feet:
the tragedy will solve itself:
there is something he does not
know.
Tragedy Andy.

I want to hold,
but you want to hold
and not be held.
I now discover I want your holding,
clear, light, a baby's embrace,
your fingers curling to my neck.
It represents, represents.

Tell him when I'm gay, I'm very gay,
with luck, to the point of ego obliteration . . .
And then what follows,
a gap, a turning, and then
another bright mansion in my father's house:
to be straight another way.

05/2012

Not All

Nothingness is not all.
It is not everything.
It is only everything
if we refuse to see it.
Then it returns to sneak upon us
like the cursing witch in
Sleeping Beauty;
excluded from the celebration,
she takes her revenge.

She wipes out entire lives
amid disease, addiction,
carelessness.
Who would have thought,
in essence
a single neurological turn
would obliterate so much,
become the hapless main course
so triumphantly,
so enthralling?
It develops edge,
we surmise,
and renders toxic.
We think, therefore
we are nothing.

We must morsel void
in every drop of mother's milk.
What confusion when

our urgency finds
the palpability of food and its reuniting handmaiden, hunger,
and seduces us into forgetting.

We are empty needing filling,
we think. Yes, but all void does not
need filling as we initially propose.
Somehow, in the interface between
flesh and flesh, can we confront
a space between,
fingers almost touching?

Is outer space itself void?
I rather think not.
Void is something else,
critical to essence,
visible and invisible –
stomach full,
taxi empty
– maybe an edgelessness
beyond our comprehension.
We can barely find the words.

04/21/2009

Our Initiation

The kiss as our initiation into separation.
To see reality in tranquility
to share it
to share responsibility with whatever God
to trust.

12/2012

Out of the Air

Most of us are born
out from the womb.
We emerge glistening
and wrinkled,
fingers long held in fluid.

Athena is born of a splitting headache,
with Hephaestes
cleaving Zeus' skull and bringing his child,
wisdom, from the god's suffering.

Even from the stork, there is
a causality to birth –
the bird carries the
weighted baby's wrap in its beak.
And does it drop the baby
down the chimney?
Some chimney.

2010

Penguins

I'm dressed fit to kill;
Black tie tuxedo, bloodless:
We dance the fox trot.

12/2007

Perfection

I know nothing quite so perfect, so clear, as a stone.
Dancing happily with a partner may be second,
I reckon,
But for solid assurance of something staying
where it is, and not moving, stones
have it.

For after all, perfection is not a matter
of an achieved state, like Massachusetts,
or singing the anthem without a mistake,
but of a way of looking at time.
Fine.

In this moment, as in all moments,
we are perfection itself, and we seek
our fates on Titanic's sloping deck,
waiting for a transition which
will hit us like an iceberg.

All is motion,
whereas the stone's movement,
substantial as it may be,
is tiny
and at our level of scanning,
largely unobservable.

The hot fudge sundae is perfection,

+

but only so long as it is eaten.
We must eat our cake to have it.

No, no swallowing rocks like Demosthenes,
mouth full of pebbles.

The stone stands still, and we are with it,
a moment of bliss,
followed by more and more
until we are transformed by stone,
and with it, alone.

9/2009

Plymouth 1986

Can we be thankful for the missed opportunities . . .
For the intimacy dropped, cut off –
For the addiction to objects,
For the dead ends of relating,
For the lack of purpose and energy,
For the pride and grandiosity flooding our consciousness,
For the venality of government,
For the undisciplined recklessness of religion,
For chores – that diddle away days.

When the Puritans came to New England,
did they arrive with such baggage?
They stepped onto the Rock
and hoped for freedom.
Half died before the year was out.
The other half faced the pain of settling into reality
and the fact that it was harder to do
something new than they thought.

When we step out at Plymouth, do we give
thanks for the opportunity to bring portions of our self together?
The intimacy achieved,
the addiction kissed goodbye,
the pleasurable companionship,
purpose, energy,
humility,
self control,
and knowledge?

2008

Reeling in the Fish

When the rod engages,
what is the site I want,
a dying fish flopping on the rowboat's floor?

More likely I want the flopping,
but I want the fish.
To love it
and have it love me back.

What will be the point?
Perhaps that is the wrong question.
How will I maintain focus,
maintain focus,
when all precognitive
sensual experience is distracting me.

This will be the task:
that it and I will embrace,
achieve rapport, that it will hold me
like a mother, or father, while our gills
engorge and subside.
A friend.

And somehow maintain focus.

Thus the desire for connection
is monolithic,
for the longest time
it does not involve two,

only one.
Coming from one, it is one.
"I want you" means "I want your company
with an undistracted, integrated me."

Reeling in the other
brings it closer
to a self which then dissolves,
disappears.

Take the hook out of its mouth, set it free
to move with me,
something so many fish cannot or will not do.
In water, they move,
so much, against.
The grid of two so complicated.
What if it says, "I want to be caught,
and by you."
How long will the dawning hours of catch and release be?
What explication, what overview will help me through the
so-called exchange?

The stations of the cross:

I take up the burden of your flesh and hold it.
You are held.
You take up my flesh, and I am held.
We aim and decide to kiss.
"May I?"
"I'd like that," you nod.
The Interface focuses and enlarges.

+

We take in more, the chemistry pulses,
catch and release.

I take the hook from your mouth,
and what remains is your longing
to remain. And the decision,
wonderful to us both,
to remain.

What other lesson plan is here?
To bond silently,
to see what being becomes when it becomes beings being.

To calculate the separation(s),
see what they involve,
the placenta peeling from its wall.
Learn something by doing, maybe.

Will it last?
Perhaps the movement across this grid will take
millions of scans to traverse;
the grid, the scanner,
we educate fast and slow.

I seek the stranger and
seek to make it a beloved,
someone I can return to
again and again – not for something else,
but for again.
And by again to mean,
to focus at the stillest point,
to bring my single awareness into another field.

I shall be its stranger,

it shall hold my strangeness and
expose me to the air.
Upside down, I shall
claim first breath,
the world's second beginning,
we are always the second beginning,
not counting times before time,
and know.

10/23/2011

Reporting Child Abuse:

There are the regular channels,
sponsored by bruises visible,
inspired by rape and assault.
Advise the supervisor,
who tells the state Department of Child Protection,
then that activates
a slow but direct process,
whereby parental patterns are
lassoed and brought down for branding;
and hopefully cessation.

Or the perpetrator
is removed from the scene,
sent to the showers
after pitching seven innings
of flawless, deeply flawed ball.

How to assess more subtle forms of abuse,
the eyebrow condescending,
the hurry up,
the implied scapegoat.
The way the perpetrator quickly turns into
perpetratee, bullied by four generations
of dysfunctionalism.
Trace the violence, not asking
the rapee whether this is what he/she wants.
It quickly muddles.

All are victims, and something

has got to stop, the tidal wave turned back
to its mother, the storm, the volcano.
If we go back, the perpetration sequence
disappears into the family tree
until you
cannot tell what branches convey what,
though you know you are doing right
by insisting that the parent take back the pattern,
pattern which does not belong to him any more
than it does to you, his child.
Can the karma be addressed in this karmic strategy?
Will it work?
Will primitive brain accept and transform under
its purvey?

7/2009

Righteousness

We don't know to start with;
to start with, we don't know.
All the lacquering of civilization
layers of knowledge, but if we approach
reality from a position of not knowing,
with no prefiguration,
a certain neural excitement
passes through our system
as we connect for the first time
with reality. This is progress.
We can approach the oldest conundra,
the Gordian knots,
and find that approached in a fresh way, they
yield, unwind,
and new oxygen courses through the tiny folds of our brains.

Progress is linked to knot knowing:
we talk about righteousness,
how difficult it is to appraise,
to line up, to fire into
for his names' sake, means not for me, but for the other.
For some superior being, something beyond ordinary
awareness.

Hard news suggests that right action is knowable,
but it is not; suicide a right action? Not sure.
Given it arises usually when things start to get better.
Not that things are worse.

10/25/2010

Sacrifice:

Sacrifice merely postpones the problem.
Let me sacrifice you on some
Impossible altar –
Or I'll disrobe, and you can place me
on the sacred platter, legs aimed high.
Whatever.
It is all a matter of getting to know you.
Me.

Maybe in the dance we shall hold the
fleeting truth fleetingly.
Or maybe we shall see that truth is
constant, constant as the Indians, who
know the future will destroy their life.
We are fleeting, egos, bodies,
The present remains the truth, right on our plate
before us.
We eat, and give thanks.

11/2014

Self and Other

I have my feelings, and the other person has theirs.
I have my tendencies, they have theirs.
If I have mine and we follow mine,
perhaps I may be met by some other
(how will I know it is an other?),
and we would be identified as compatible:
which means
you can also play your record on my machine.
Which is suited
or is illusioned.
Why do I want another reality,
where your separateness
is then bridge
over which I cross;
that I need is not just the same
but the difference.
What happens when we unzip?

7/2009

Snow

Jesus is swaddled in snow.
Out of control,
how quickly we master everything
but the essential.

What if I were to awake
and be the presence
under the trees,
white, blinding,
apparently unmoving,
but clearly only one locus
of water's potentiality.

In other seasons
we shall have liquid,
vapor.
These lie awaiting.

Michael is nearby
witnessing the truth
with me,
not crying out, or laughing,
or exploding.
We merely sit.
Shall we be as silent as the snow,
with spikey stars soothed
into a calm, undulating

+

surface?

He shall leave soon –
and so shall I,
heading for separate Christmases,
different icy flakes,
linked only from the highest
perspective where it is true:
we are of the same.

Particles and waves,
an undulating sea
crystalized into fantastic,
airbrushed landscape,
concealing and revealing,
cold and vibrant and welcoming,
enthralling as reality.

What can I do for you?
What can I do with you?
Already the link has been forged,
and now what is there to do?

12/23/2008

Snow2

Snow, man is no man,
Who shall kiss the mistletoe?
You miss the point, man.

12/2008

Snow, Stevens-style

Snowman is no man;
Who shall kiss the mistle toe?
You miss the point, man.

                                                                      12/23/2008

Spider Plant

Arachnoid tendrils
Hover over. I wonder:
Shall we kiss the floor?

7/10/2015

Stairs

I missed a stair.
The floor
Rushing up,
My legs,
Destined to climb,
Stammer at the riser.
The things I am holding
A canvas tote,
Some clothes,
Today's mail –
Fall unceremoniously
Around my catapulting,
Reversing bulk.
I hit my head
On a rounded edge of
Wood, a juxtaposition rarely
Experienced, now fully
My reality.

Thrown down,
Torquing
Like a jazz improvisation
Late at night – going
Somewhere, nowhere.
Damn, I cry, to the
Devil who made me do it,
Itself a wanderer, filled
With inattention.
What was stored at the side

Of the head also limps
Down to the landing, in lots
And inevitability.

I burl
On its edge, my pelvis
Jarred – a happy parade
Stopped abruptly by a
Sniper shooting all the
Instruments and instrument
Carriers to the ground.

Perfection means following
Gravity accurately –
A missed step casts me
Far above, below reality, and
I hurt.

The pain is one thing,
My aging, already prepared for
Decades ago, each cell
Vanquished,
Is another.

5/2009

Television

You do not call after you promised to.
You merely repeat.
I wonder where you are, what
corners of your neurochemistry you are
trapped by, unable to bring your
finger to the cellphone screen.
Fear of what it means, you and I,
fear of breaking taboos ancient and
incorrigible. You are an artist but that
does not wheel out enough courage for
you to declare yourself with me, for yourself.
You have already declared yourself with me, for me.
The mother hovers, father sleeps, in
death and in life.
We must move beyond soap and
sitcom to find a new place where we can
rest, no longer actors, but action,
trusting our radiance.
Everything points to this possibility.
I seek a lover, person present;
We shall conjoin.
Let's turn our turbid teacher television off.

2005

Thanksgiving 08

Each layer approached
reveals an additional arena
for mastery –
a differentiation of perception
by the differentiating brain.

Who is to say how this works:
the instrument of perception
yielding – what? – shall we call it
knowledge
of increasingly
separate pieces.

It has taken years (ha!)
to manifest what the Greeks intuited
about an ultimate, irreducible
particle,
and even that atomic understanding
yields
to subatomic realities.

Is the division endless –
in us,
and in the world?
Do our brains thus commit
to fluidity,
even as the neurological tracks

+

are laid down
upon which the engine rolls?
In a sense, we never learn.
Let us give thanks
for this adept responsiveness,
God within God,
which is what we are.

11/2008

The Birds Die

In Angel Memorial
the birds live and die only;
no birds are born here.

Pet-serving hospitals
serve pets and pet owners.
Regular human hospitals
serve people and their families.

Systems serve systems which
include the designated patient,
the pet or parent.
(Not to mention the staff and their families.)

A grandparent seeks the
aid of oxygen and bedpans
and morphine.
The child dies, the world dies,
the bird brain does not fathom
what is safe and what is not.
It turns out my grace-filled surgeon
drives me home one day after my operation
because the hospital
is filled with dangerous germs;
we never thought about it like that before now.

The birds die;

+

so far, I do not quite.
I am safe, but so now are the
birds who died.

                                                                  6/2009

The Day the Universe Changed

The day the universe changed
the sky was bright blue,
sun torquing every molecule of air
into its radiance.

I, in a depression you could not
push with a plow, walked
out from my house and
saw the trees.

They stood upright,
transforming CO_2 into oxygen
(were the leaves separating
the carbon molecules with their tiny
fingers and laying them out
in rows, like chocolates, for assimilation later?);

and I only saw them partially,
saw their greens, their magnificence,
their turgor uprightness, and extension,
their cleverness, their wisdom,
their usefulness, their essentiality.

But I did not see their mystery.
I was caught in a depth with their beauty
but not their unknowingness.

+

I thought I knew, but I did not.
Surely, I ventured, God does not not know.
She knows, dammit.

But God does not know. God is mystery
unto itself, and we are its wake,
spuming off divine Evinrudes at the
back of the boat, plowing.

Here's change, I thought, change of
some magnitude.

10/2000

The depressed see things as they are.

We are comfortable with the way things are,
the gate leading to our grandmother's house,
porridge,
the automobile which shifts clutchless with polished buttons.
An electric toothbrush charging high above my bathroom sink.
I teach about empathic perception
and how that is the highest form of perception:
we see the Other as from within the Other, unobstructed,
undistorted by stammering narcissism.

But what, I ask, are the encumbrances
to empathy, and I find myself saying,
they are the encumbrances to the third eye,
seeing inwards upon the self.

What if that were the whole of education's purpose,
to clear the third eye, so that
it can see inward, and thus see outward.
This is how we eliminate projection,
for now there is no need.
We see wholly because we are whole.

This is how we record history, read history:
Where is the clarity, the transcendence
beyond identity, and its tiny variegations
within religion and race and nationality?

+

Best not to trust those billboard organizers for any truth.
I look for neighbors who want to dance with me,
Our dance is variations of solos.

10/2001

The Epiphany

I supposed the assignment is doomed from the start:
find a poem relating to epiphany.
Right off, I couldn't think of any.
"Kubla Khan"? Ecstatic, but not really epiphantic.

We check the internet definitions, and
they cluster after this fashion:

the vivid experience of an unusual insight,
usually prepared for or ruminated about before,
when enlightenment about some problem or other
occurs, and we see old things in a new way,
in an unprepared sort of way.

Well, there are lots of descriptions of epiphany occasions,
including eureka,
or somehow relating to finding long lost keys underneath the seat,
or realizing that we are mistaken in persecuting the early Christian sectaries,
and we connect to that portion in our chemistry which
has lots of serotonin and we are the Christ
we have been cruelly repressing.

It is all about projection and encapsulation:
what takes us beyond our dissociated self-limiting
boundaries involving what we think of as self.
Eureka, the Berlin Wall falls,

+

and we are invited to live transcendently in Germany.

Well, epiphany has its arousal and its detumescent risks.
The moment of transformation, even conversion,
reveals the predominant
undertow power of dissociation.
Before we were in the dark;
now, lightbulb, we are in the light.
In the subsequent cascade of insight,
our brain realigns into revised vision of
a situation, and emotion, a problem: reality.
Unlocked, unknotted, integrated.

– only it's sometimes hard to sustain:
afterward, we may return to the familiar,
only we hope with some residual afterburn.
Sometimes we shed our clothes
and walk naked upon the streets,
streets now also naked.

Who records in poetry the moment itself?
Hard to say. Usually an epiphany poem
is a reporting of the recollected moment,
not the inspiration itself; that is
beyond words; beyond images.
Ian thinks pretty much all poems recall, describe, evoke epiphanies.
I like that.
I recall a therapeutic moment when Peter told me to look at a visualized black,
and he said, "The shock energy is stored (storied) in the black",
and slowly/instantaneously but demonstrably
my selfview transformed, and my worldview,

which had been preparing for years,
changed with it, forever.
(At least I have been sustaining it ever since;
to varying degrees of integration.)

I practition with a client psychiatrist,
and in a single moment,
he feels a significant worldselfview change –
he has gotten what he hoped and paid for;
and each following session,
he longs for me to evoke similar transformation,
like some everynight Scheherezade:
a thousand preparatory occasions until the calif's
tyrannical heart epiphaneously declares, "I give up. I shall marry you."
I suppose there are small epiphanies and earthshaking ones.

Depending on what kind of sneezing, seizing, we are prone to experience.

And there are Zen paradoxes which will force the bud, as it were,
as one spectrumed brain section connects with another.

That's it:
Where do we go after epiphany?
We dwell with the new insight
and consolidate it,
refer to its lesson in memory,
as I have done.

Let its light flow to trillions of cells,

+

illuminating and
reestablishing a correct and humble view of myself,
knowing and not knowing.
The center finds itself, declares itself genius,
and then still must brush its new, and old teeth,
or with its new mouth, speak a new language.
Somehow, we want the epiphaneous moment,
unexpected as it may initially appear to be, to extend.

Epiphanies can be sudden or drawn out, but the ones usually reported
describe some movement in the brain, experienced as exceptional –
of greater velocity or turbulence.
Three days ago, Kevin characterized epiphany musically as a moment violent and chaotic, but
I think it also simultaneously moves with less randomness.

Perhaps as we scan, epiphany evens out into a glow, a relief,
a sense that at last, we are commensurate with divinity,
our mind, our brain sufficient to perceive reality
and act accordingly.

Epiphany is linked with our traumata and their resolution.
Some initiating shock is reworked, and for a moment
or series of moments, our brain bounces back and forth
and comes to a glowing rest, into clear.
Our cognitive and emotional traffic can now appear to resume its flow,
or cease altogether: the promise of conversion, of brain change, is fulfilled,
and we can feel it and watch it unfold.
In the electronic burst, time itself is transformed, and we with it.

One trouble is
it is happening always,
and in our stillest silence,
always here,
and it is happening now.

01/06/2015

The Picnic

I try to bring everything.
The sandwiches already made
so I don't have to carry bread and jars
of peanut butter and jelly
or ham and cheese
and mayonnaise.

There is a pile of
stuff in the kitchen and refrigerator
I am not bringing along.
I have left them all behind.

What else:
Forget not ice, nor napkins, nor something to drink.
Picnics are when a bit snail-like, I can
take my home provisions
with me, and carry them
to a place which is food barren.

05/10/2012

The Water Moved

The water moved with the wind,
bright blue turning
white and grey
with wide short
black stripes in the valleys
of the waves.

The face of the clock is
still;
black antique fingers pass
over entombed numerals, sweeping
the air high above the
dial's flat white paint.

Love works like these,
sweeping with fingers
above the still, winding clock face
until the water moves.

11/1999

The World is But an Instant

The world is but an instant,
conceived and executed,
begun and beginning,
finishing and concluded.
We are but spanners, holding its crush
apart,
the compressor paused for Eden's void
to flash before our eyes.

It shows up in the focus I have
for each moment:
now I am hunting the void,
happy in that;
that is what I want to see, not
the staging which holds up its walls.
I was not supposed to look, to see;
why have others conspired to
encourage me so?
Disencourage.
Discourage.

So I see (sew eye sea)
each moment is focused upon the
center which holds;
it is in the middle of everything.
No matter which way I glance.
I shall not dart my eyes,
voluntarily or involuntarily,
drawn to some distracting

vibration which promises substance.
Only void will do.

My nephew Ian studies eye movement
for marketers trying to determine what
we look at as we enter a store.
My eye movements are flushed with centers,
points of focus which now
instead of wandering, stabilize.
Some permission is being given.
Some center will be not evaded.

And will I, as the stories go,
fall into this center,
subsumed
in some kind of self-immolation?

For my remaining years, I
will face the center,
fall into it regularly in a regarded
self-immolation.
Its speed and density will increase
my range, enabling me to
to go farther out, if I want to.
This appears to be my plan, happy in letting go
to all that is not the center.
A happiness of sorts.

05/2014

The Worse It Gets

It gets worse, the worse it gets.
I began carrying my own cross up
the hill, thorns scraping my eyebrows, and
the bugs biting my ankles.

When will this stop – The Vilification;
The Calumny; The Projections?
I think:
All I want is to bring relief from suffering,
only, sticking my head above the trenches as I have,
I get nailed.

God, give me strength to overcome projective identification.
No, just endure it.
What is its jungle purpose?

Hasn't anyone heard that we do unto others what we do to
ourselves?
What is the lesson here?
Trudge, trudge.
Is there an end to this?

Gimme a break. I would like everyone
on this road to stop this sadism for just a minute and take a
deep breath.
We are all being too self-aggrandizing, too self-dramatizing
here.
It speaks of lack of self-knowledge, to say the least.

10/1991

This Space is New

This space is new,
glistening with white mud exudite,
trembling.

Its edge is catastrophic,
with no surveyor synapses
to identify its, what,
shall I say, limits.

It's an Herculean task,
and I lie back and watch
the, what, shall I say,
top – flat and bright,
with sounds below, far below.

Swaddling does not help,
nor the almost Internet –
I must move a hand,
an arm, simulating birth,
but this is new, this space.

The motions of the day
have been steady enough,
over decades,
offices
practiced and practical.
New space is a freedom

+

desired, feared,
disorienting, and
I don't know what it will do to me;
how the new space
will make it impossible
to cut my toenails
in an old way.

Is there a connection
between space and specificity?
We evolve into 60% water, and
we are always ½ space.
Symphonies, we rush through
silence like revolving doors –
do we do the same with space?

Decompression brings
joy and
wistful sadness –
so much history transformed
gently or quickly
obliterated in fade out
or dissolve.

My blanket holds, returns
my heat.
This new space holds
my space
and does not return.

2/15/2013

12.5 Ways of Looking at a Blackboard

1.
I know flourescent light hits the floor
with almost the same intensity
as it does the desktop.
One light year.

2.
The carpet will absorb the sound
that chalk makes.
In discussion,
we turn away.

3.
Books line the walls.
Computers hum,
civilization's crucible.
What, within invisibility,
goes on here?

4.
There are four bodies here,
three students, one teacher:
i.e., four teachers, four students.
That makes eight,
plus personalities,
plus medications.

+

5.
As nominal teacher
I lead the class.
The anominal teacher
darts between insights,
flying between sentences,
words, nanoclefts.
After a while,
books cease to help.

6.
We fill the room with talk.
We fill the room with silence.
There is movement and no movement.
Same moment.

7.
We all have feet.
We sit with our legs under the desks,
beneath the light.
Our desks face the center of the room.

8.
I cannot count past twelve;
this is multi-tasking
carried to absurdity.
Better to litter me home
with the medals I have already acquired,
high and flat on my supine chest.

9.
We are on our own,
out past the float.

Regard our neurons racing to garner
one focal point out of a casual list of
apparently random brainscraps
assembled (in Hartford?),
prior to anything wingéd,
a chaotic corner turned, and suddenly
the darkest, safest feathered magic bullet: "Look,"
he says, "I found it first."
Symbols are not wrought:
magnets promising faith,
they are likewise gathered
by roadside prisoners
with point sticks and collecting bags.
Men and women of Belmont,
behold how, little, we know.
A good day,
we swim beyond analysis.

10.
I have no idea where our conversation rests,
no synapse-specific site.
Time stops and keeps on going.
Memory sports a nursing bra.
I become an odd fundamentalist.

11.
History proffers a start,
a clearing in the woods
with a few stumps standing.
We try to master if then now and then.

+

12.
Let me be clear about this:
how great is my luck
to see what I see,
feel what I feel.

12.5
Let's figure this thing out.

06/2009

Unsacerdotal Vision

I see the world better when I am wearing glasses.
I go to the drug store
hoping for an assisted clarity,
and each time I buy something new.
I know I see the world better
when I am wearing glasses,
because I do.
Only recently I have been trying different
glass tints, various wedge form frames
varying depths for astigmatism;

and it does not seem to matter.
No matter what my new glasses,
for a time I see better.
Even those eyeglasses made for the near-blind,
with bottle-thick lenses
work.

Systems are like that.
For a time they render reality
until through wear, tear, familiarity,
they are outgrown,
they become scratch-decadent
to the native eye,
they no longer serve
to bring the sharp need for focus to our yearning.

+

Each new pair of glasses brings a reformation,
and while I know I will not see as well without them,
I long for the unobstructed view,
the unfiltered, unmitigated reality.
Unsacerdotal vision.
But somehow, that goal no longer applies.
I have been instructed in systems,
shown how to use them
and sometimes how they can be abused,
and in turn, abuse.
They protect, enhance, and unhappily, limit.

Our inner eye sometimes cannot see,
and so our outer vision is compromised.
And so we need glasses to compensate
for eye alignment already declaring an
inner vision problem.
The correction is second hand,
and our desire only temporarily sated.

Every eye open is an occasion for awe.

10/2010

Vacation

I wish you a Merry Christmas
and a Happy New Year.
My present to myself is to
pass out from containment

into freedom. Giving and
receiving matters so little
on the broad scale.
I resent their flourishes.

Rather, let me sit with
a friend, in the deepest
silence, to watch the rising snow.

I shall give up the past
and, like Jesus,
face the Crucifiction,
located a few twisting inches away
from the Manger.
Mange.

Away from the Manger
no crypt for a bed,

learning possible, not rote,
and lion sits down with the goat.
They already do: I mean the kill

+

between animals is struggle, but not too much pain.
Norepinephrin.

Returning to the learning.
My heart takes its aim,
and swaddles the hurt,
not knowing how to do anything more.

Let me hold you and watch
the healing unfold.
We are here to do that.
In Jesus' sad name.

12/2009

Vaccination

If you want the pattern to change,
don't call it evil.
If you dislike the situation,
don't call it evil.
If you want the behavior concluded,
don't call it evil.
By its holder, thus named,
it cannot be understood:
there is no wiggle room.
If we cannot understand,
we cannot change.

Within the identification of evil
as such
resides a despair, a hapless resignation,
a defiant sense that we have the discipline to
view the thing and name it,
set its limits,
provide an essentially historical
beginning, middle, and end to the phenomenon,
mirroring the attempt of the enthralled, violating brain to
do the same.
Naming evil is mirroring the phenomenon
which promulgates our naming.
That is all.

Here, we'll set a final solution,

+

and promulgate a series of
commensurate behaviors,
each having its own phenomenal reality and
all too recognizable aftershocks.

Do not characterize something or someone Satanic
unless you want the system to perpetuate.
We cannot learn from the tyrant unless we
see clearly, warts and all,
see to the point where maybe care
has not been taken,
some verb not fully parsed,
and some deeper truth is
being avoided,
over and over again.
Otherwise we have learned nothing.

There is a pivot place within the chemistry,
a probably sacred vibratory state when all the
static and dissonance resolve, and
we surrender into whatever: compassion, love, enlightenment –
and we do not generate the gestures,
the activities, which would be called evil.
From that centered place,
we are righteous,
and we commit true actions.

Perhaps we can even conclude
the badness which we feel internally.
But evil is beyond shame,
and we must put aside shame
if we are to see evil
wearing its ultimate cloak, and so

ask it to disrobe.
Though it is hard to tell.

Because of the way our brains work,
if we strike a higher vibration, in ourselves
or near others, we can evoke the worst trauma sites –
seeking resolution –
cast somewhat in the direction of the stimulus
which sets them off.
We don't have to be bad to set off the bad patterns:
we can be very good.

We set the patterns off.
With evil in our hand,
we can command attention,
like a watchman crying out "Fire!",
but it is not just that.
Once sending the message of distress,
a set of predictable and usually ineffective
measures are set in motion,
like war being declared,
and then we are into war, and not
into vaccinating against the occasions which
set war off.

It is the naming wherein evil
lies, but it has no attributes,
no Satanic envy.
There will be a time when
people will laugh evil off the stage,
like a false prophet,

+

promising resolution when there can be none.
Now evil is endless.

Naming something evil is the thing itself.

I am in dialogue with my parents,
always attempting to resolve,
explain, balance
the contradictions of their thought and being,
vis-a-vis me in relationship to them or in relation to themselves.
My respect for them precludes
sometimes the concerns other people have
when they determine what is important and what is not.
I am still trying to solve some conundrum
which they could not.

I recall a Quaker meeting
where someone stood up and
stressed the difference between the
Mennonites and the other Quakers,
as if this long – what was it, conflict?
was still important.

To her it was, yet to me it
it had no meaning.
For her, it was some higher order of
understanding she was appealing to, in contradistinction to
what her mother said the other people
were thinking.
She was upholding, or modifying the understanding
for a recalcitrant, or misunderstood parent,
explaining the importance
which if I knew what she was talking about,

probably would be my understanding too.
But I didn't have time to ask her why it was important.
Perhaps there was some hidden antagonist in the Friends meeting
who needed reminding that they would not get away with it.
Whatever it was they had gotten away with.

I adjust my thinking to accommodate to their expertise:
there, here is the trail, and this is the best way
to traverse it. Ice below, watch out.

Or I set my own course, recalling their spills,
their falls.
Often I am far beyond where they ski,
but usually somewhere on the same slopes.

We progress and we do not.
The family system progresses
and it does not.
The civilization progresses,
and it does not.

I measure the distance I "progress" in each move I make from
its declared narrative back to the still center from which
it begins.

2009

Valentine's Day

This morning it is zero, but the sun is out.
70 years ago today,
10 gangsters were massacred in a Chicago
garage, the blood flowed dark heart red
from advanced monkeys all,
staining a concrete floor.
It is hard to put that memory into workable perspective.

Now we send our Valentines
across the seas,
toward counterdirectional Easts –
where does East begin? –
to Juliet,
the sun:
racing past her Mediterranean
warmth, a rose of death,
coyly calibrating her sweetness before its demise.

Perhaps day's flight expresses
a mere steady overarching:
we turn our heads
to watch her
settling gently into set.
In spite of pooled, drained, liquid from within,
she holds our hearts, our eyes,
our concrete hearts.

05/2011

Watch

Casios need no
winding. But food's the trick to
keep time ticking.

Copied 06/1998

Windows

Endowed with clarity,
the window is both hard and
final.
It is a cell wall,
firm, yet allowing some
information to be exchanged.
We see out, we see in,
we are protected from the
wind, or we are the wind,
unable to come inside.

The window is not the cell wall. It is in this
way rigid, inflexible,
shatterable. It channels
light, but is itself
at some macro level unmoved.

The window is ego,
standing between,
a mediatrix
transducing.

High in a window sill,
a prism
fractionates the sunlight into a preverbal
rainbow, doling color
upon the wooden floor.

I will extend myself beyond the

center of my cells,
right up to the wall,
where I can see.

Winter 1998

What's In A Name?

I sweep my dirt floor,
stepsisters complain so bad:
I'm Cinderella.

12/2009

Without hands

Without hands the ocean soars
amid twinkling cranial shores,
passing through their surface,
until substance becomes only sensation.

Pulsations have a deeper intelligence
than thought,
No apparent suffering nor pain,
no holding – even pattern
within the waves –
an interested God,
toying with Its child,
synapses.

I am stilled by the movement,
something for a time separate
from my island me,
like a corner dustball,
thriving in the wind.

Enthralled, I watch, then watch
again;
how many times do my eyes watch,
then cast away, or down, then gaze again –
the surf passes over the familiar beaches,
quickly taking everything with it in a
surge which carries cars and flat limbs of gas stations

+

in its forearm sweep across the highway
up and around the high-rises,
swamping their basements.

I sink, therefore I am.
The lighthouse beam is coursing
yet clearly unobservant,
its consistency
constant.

Like an happy dream,
the tsunami reestablishes
what is important,
which is to say almost nothing;
yet without it,
we are lost,
importunate and feckless.

It subsides,
and what is left are
small skirmishes,
an overall extension of range, scope,
where what might have been damage
is perceived as congruent,
happily alone.

02/2016

You and I return

I am speaking
Into the void.
Who, if it disappears – does that mean forever?
Or is there a cloud
above which
remembers?
I face the void with
centered attention
What I say
stays for human time.

02/20/2013

Contents

Against Incarnation | 3
Almost 69 | 7
Already Love | 14
As the Wind Blows | 15
At Once | 16
Be | 17
Behind the Moon | 19
Betrayal | 22
Be-trayal | 23
Beyond | 25
Butterflies Fill the Sky | 28
Calligraphy | 30
Changing Tires on Lunchbreak | 31
Dan the Treeman | 32
Dislocation | 38
Don't Fuck With Me | 40
First Day of School | 41
Getting Naked With the Teacher | 42
Halloween 2013 | 45
Halloween 2014: 6 for the day | 47
Halloween Stuff | 48
The Dead | 49
I Have No Clue | 51
Pumpkin | 52
I Wake | 53
He Took | 54

I Come Into the World
to Touch / 56
Icon / 57
I Lay My Flesh Down / 63
I'm Good With My Hands / 65
Hell and Forever / 66
I Now See / 67
I Wonder How / 69
Last Crisis / 72
Leave Taking / 75
Left Over / 76
Left Over Annex / 78
Light Change (a portion) / 79
Mary Weeps / 80
Musée / 83
Must I / 88
Not All / 90
Our Initiation / 92
Out of the Air / 93
Penguins / 94
Perfection / 95
Plymouth 1986 / 97
Reeling in the Fish / 98
Reporting Child Abuse: / 102
Righteousness / 104
Sacrifice: / 105
Self and Other / 106
Snow / 107
Snow2 / 109
Snow, Stevens-style / 110
Spider Plant / 111
Stairs / 112
Television / 114

Thanksgiving 08 / 115
The Birds Die / 117
The Day the Universe Changed / 119
The depressed see things as they are. / 121
The Epiphany / 123
The Picnic / 128
The Water Moved / 129
The World is But an Instant / 130
The Worse It Gets / 132
This Space is New / 133
12.5 Ways of Looking at a Blackboard / 135
Unsacerdotal Vision / 139
Vacation / 141
Vaccination / 143
Valentine's Day / 148
Watch / 149
Windows / 150
What's In A Name? / 152
Without hands / 153
You and I return / 155